A Special Anthology Recipes from Games of Thrones

The Flavors of Seven Kingdoms

By - Rene Reed

Copyright © 2021 Rene Reed.

License Notes

All rights reserved. No part of this book may be reproduced in any form except permitted by the author. You may use brief excerpts of this book in published reviews. The author shall not be responsible for damages resulting from the reader's use of the contents of this book.

Table of Contents

Introduction 6

Appetizers, drinks 8

    Arya Stark's Oyster soup 9

    Seven Kingdoms Honey and Milk Potion 12

    Almond Butter Honey Smoothie 14

    Hot chocolate with cinnamon 16

    Sweet pumpkin soup with maple sugar 18

    Vegetable soup 20

    Creamy spinach soup 22

Breakfasts 24

    Hot Pie's DireWolf Bread 25

    Bowl of brown 27

    Black bread 30

    Cheesy bacon and egg hash 32

    Breakfast strata 34

    Egg and cottage cheese breakfast bowl 36

- Main course 38
  - Meat pie 39
  - Tourtiere 42
  - Lamb stew 45
  - Arya Stark's Crab and Lobsters with Mushrooms 48
  - Fried Crab Claws 50
  - Creamy fish stew 52
  - Fish pie 55
  - Turnip Greens Stew 58
  - Cersei's Creamy Chestnut soup 60
  - White beans and bacon 63
  - Mushroom Pie 66
- Desserts 69
  - Lemon cake 70
  - Cersei's War Feast Cheesecake 72
  - Apple pie 74
  - Mini marzipan cakes 76
  - Cherry tarts 79

 Cream Snow Cupcakes 81

Conclusion 84

About the Author 85

Author's Afterthoughts 86

Introduction

Horse heart and Dragon Eggs may not sound very appetizing but this is not all we see in Games of Thrones as food. There are lots of dishes which are perfectly appetizing and all the GOT fans want to try them. We have brought you all the gourmet recipes which you have seen in this legendary story.

Games of Thrones has made and broke many records across the world and the fans are gone crazy over it. The GOT craze is everywhere and food is no exception. The fans want to arrange parties with the Games of Throne theme and cook foods from the series to relive those beautiful memories.

We have made it all easy for you! This special cookbook is a complete guide to arrange any type of food for your Game of Thrones party. We have covered special drinks, appetizing starters, exclusive breakfasts, mouthwatering main course, and luxurious desserts for you.

Pick any recipe from this cookbook to make your ordinary family gathering into a special GOT court. We suggest you add some signature décor items to complete the atmosphere. You are free to use any recipe from here to make your picky eaters some healthy, home-made food with GOT twist.

Appetizers, drinks

Arya Stark's Oyster soup

Arya Stark goes on a mission to finish the Thin Man disguised as Lanna. She pretends to be a shellfish seller in Braavos. Let's taste this mouthwatering oyster soup to cherish the adventurous mission of our brave lady. The strong taste and aroma are sure to accelerate your appetite.

Serving size: 6

Cooking time: 1 hour

Ingredients:

- Chopped button mushrooms ½ cup
- All-purpose flour ¼ cup
- Bay leaf 1
- Cayenne pepper ½ teaspoon
- Dried sage ¼ teaspoon
- Finely chopped onion ½ cup
- Chicken broth 4 cups
- Shucked oysters and juice 12
- Dried thyme ¼ teaspoon
- Dried oregano ¼ teaspoon
- Drained artichoke hearts 1 can
- Butter ½ cup
- Salt ¾ teaspoon
- Butter 2 tablespoons
- Heavy cream 1 cup
- Finely chopped carrot ½ cup
- Finely chopped celery ½ cup

Instructions:

Sauté fresh mushrooms, celery, onion, and chopped carrots in 2 tablespoons butter in a pot until onions become transparent and soft.

Melt half cup butter in a pot and stir in flour. Cook for about 5 minutes.

Whisk in chicken broth in the flour mixture.

Add the sage, oregano, thyme, cayenne pepper, salt, bay leaf, artichokes, and sautéed vegetables. Simmer for about 20 minutes on medium heat.

Whisk in the cream. Add the oysters. Simmer the mixture but don't boil. Pour it in the soup bowls and serve hot.

Seven Kingdoms Honey and Milk Potion

Honey in cold milk was the drink we saw many characters drinking in this mind-blowing series. Making this drink is very easy but we wanted to break the stereotype. Here is our upgraded version of cold milk with honey for you. The richness of coconut, pineapple, and vanilla makes it a perfect fit for everyone.

Serving size: 1

Cooking time: 10 minutes

Ingredients:

- Water ½ cup
- Honey 1 tablespoon or more if needed
- Ice cubes ½ cup
- Pineapple chunks ½ cup
- Reduced-fat coconut milk ½ cup
- Vanilla whey protein powder 1 scoop

Instructions:

Combine the vanilla protein powder, honey, ice, chunks of pineapple, coconut milk, and water in the blender.

Blend for about 2 minutes and until smooth.

Pour the smoothie into a glass and serve.

Almond Butter Honey Smoothie

Almonds and nuts are the two foods that were very popular among the people of medieval times. We have used almond butter and honey to make this ultra-rich, creamy drink. You may take it as a quick energizer or serve it to the guests in your Games of Thrones party.

Serving size: 1

Cooking time: 5 minutes

Ingredients:

- Almond butter ¼ cup
- Almond milk 1 ½ cups
- Ground cinnamon 1 tablespoon
- Honey 2 tablespoons
- Chopped frozen banana 1

Instructions:

Blend the cinnamon, honey, almond butter, and almond milk in the blender until smooth.

Add banana to it and blend again for 2 minutes.

Pour the smoothie into a glass and serve.

Hot chocolate with cinnamon

The cold and chilly winters of the icy North were not an easy task for the Dragons who were the leading characters from the kingdom. We have brought a solution to this problem for everyone. Just like the characters of the Games of Thrones, kick away the cold with this hot chocolate. Cinnamon adds a yummy and flavorful twist to your regular mug of hot chocolate.

Serving size: 1

Cooking time: 5 minutes

Ingredients:

- Whole milk 1 cup
- Sugar 2 tablespoons
- Unsweetened cocoa powder 2 tablespoons
- Ground cinnamon a pinch
- Freshly grated nutmeg a pinch
- Salt one pinch
- Milk chocolate chips 1 tablespoon

Instructions:

Take a mug and add the nutmeg, cinnamon, salt, chocolate, sugar, and cocoa powder to it.

Add milk to a pot and bring it to a simmer on medium heat.

Remove it from the heat and transfer it to a mug.

Stir it until all the ingredients get incorporated well. It will take almost 1 minute. Enjoy the hot chocolate.

Sweet pumpkin soup with maple sugar

Arya, Sansa, and Ned enjoyed a pleasant-looking pumpkin soup when they had dinner in King's Landing. What can be better than savoring the hot, creamy pumpkin soup in front of a fireplace watching your favorite series? This unique and heavenly tasty recipe is all you need to warm yourself up on the cold winter nights. Serve it as a snack or make it a part of your menu for special gatherings.

Serving size: 4

Cooking time: 40 minutes

Ingredients:

- Butter 2 tablespoons
- Minced garlic cloves 2
- Diced large sweet onion 1
- Vegetable stock 4 cups
- Salt 2 teaspoons
- Pumpkin puree 4 cups
- Fresh nutmeg ¼ teaspoon
- Heavy cream ¼ cup
- Maple sugar 1 tablespoon and more for garnishing as needed

Instructions:

Heat butter in a stockpot.

Sauté onion on medium heat for 5 minutes and until it becomes soft.

Add garlic to it and cook for 2 minutes and until fragrant.

Add the nutmeg, salt, maple sugar, stock, and pumpkin puree in the pot slowly.

Bring the ingredients of the pot to boiling, then decrease the heat. Simmer for half an hour and until soup coats on the spoon back.

Turn the heat off and add the heavy cream. Puree it using the stand blender or immersion until smooth.

Pour the soup into the bowls. Garnish using the maple sugar.

Vegetable soup

Vegetable soups have been a very common food in the middle ages. We are not sure what were the ingredients and recipe of those soups but try our recipe of vegetable soup. We have recreated this healthy, aromatic, and spicy recipe for you. Let's try it!

Serving size: 6

Cooking time: 30 minutes

Ingredients:

- Chicken broth 1 can
- Sliced carrots 2
- Diced large potato 1
- Chopped fresh green beans 1 cup
- Diced celery stalks 2
- Salt and pepper to taste
- Diced tomatoes 1 can
- Tomato-vegetable juice cocktail 1 can
- Fresh corn kernels 1 cup
- Creole seasoning to taste
- Water 1 cup

Instructions:

Combine the corn, green beans, chopped tomatoes, celery, carrots, potatoes, water, tomato juice, and broth in a big stockpot.

Season it with the creole, pepper, and salt.

Bring the mixture to boiling. Simmer for half an hour and until the vegetables become tender.

Creamy spinach soup

If you prefer a richer, creamier texture for your soups, here is the recipe. Taking inspiration from the vegetable soups popular in medieval times, we have created this recipe with special ingredients. This easy to make recipe will be your new favorite for sure.

Serving size: 5

Cooking time: 45 minutes

Ingredients:

- Water 2 cups
- Garlic powder ¼ teaspoon
- All-purpose flour ¼ cup
- Chopped onion ½ cup
- Thawed frozen chopped spinach 1 lb.
- Half-and-half 3 cups
- Pepper and salt to taste
- Butter ¼ cup
- Chicken bouillon granules 4 teaspoons

Instructions:

Place the spinach, garlic powder, water, onion, and bouillon in a pot on medium heat.

Bring the ingredients to boiling and decrease the heat to medium. Simmer until the onion becomes tender.

Meanwhile, put the butter in a saucepan on heat to melt. Whisk in flour until it becomes smooth.

Cook the mixture for about 2 minutes and add half-and-half slowly.

Pour the mixture of cream into the soup. Simmer it for 10 minutes and until thickened.

Season the soup with pepper and salt to taste.

Breakfasts

Hot Pie's DireWolf Bread

Made by Hot Pie, the chubby, orphan baker made the wolf pie, which Arya ate while on an escape with Hot Pie and Gendry. Our version of Direwolf bread is an improvised version that carries our years of experience in cooking. Don't worry if you are a starter in cooking. This recipe is simple and the perfect choice to make a GOT breakfast.

Serving size: 12

Cooking time: 1 hour 20 minutes

Ingredients:

- Buttermilk 1/3 cup
- White sugar 1 ½ cups
- Baking soda 1 teaspoon
- All-purpose flour 1 ¾ cups
- Mashed bananas 1 cup
- Beaten eggs 2
- Salt ½ teaspoon
- Vegetable oil ½ cup
- Chopped pecans ½ cup (optional)

Instructions:

Preheat the oven to about 325 F.

Spray a loaf pan of about 9x5 inches using the non-stick spray.

Blend the bananas, oil, buttermilk, and eggs in a bowl.

Sift the salt, baking soda, flour, and sugar together. Add it to the mixture of banana, then stir in the pecans. Mix them well.

Pour the mixture into the loaf pan. Bake for 1 hour 20 minutes. Serve.

Bowl of brown

We have been talking about all the recipes made and enjoyed by the royals in Game of Thrones. The poor and people outside the monarchy had humble meals too. For all the GOT fans, this recipe is inspired by the bowl of brown in the series. Originally, it was a staple stew in the Flea Bottom district of King's Landing. We have made up a similar recipe which is sweet in taste and contains all the healthy ingredients.

Serving size: 10

Cooking time: 1 hour

Ingredients:

- Quick-cooking oats 7 cups
- Brown sugar ½ cup
- Vegetable oil ½ cup
- Wheat bran 1 cup
- Wheat germ 1 cup
- Honey ½ cup
- Ground nutmeg 1 teaspoon
- Flaked coconut 1 cup
- Water ½ cup
- Ground cinnamon 1 teaspoon
- Chopped dates 1 cup
- Salt 1 teaspoon
- Chopped pecans 1 cup
- Vanilla extract 1 tablespoon

Instructions:

Preheat the oven to about 275 F and mix the wheat bran, wheat germ, and mixed oats in a big bowl.

Blend water, honey, vegetable oil, and brown sugar in another bowl.

Mix in the salt, nutmeg, cinnamon, and vanilla extract.

Put the mixture of brown sugar into the mixture of oat until it becomes moist uniformly. Then, transfer the mixture into a shallow but big baking dish.

Bake in the preheated oven for at least 45 minutes until it becomes light brown in color. Keep stirring after 15 minutes.

Mix coconut, pecans, and dates in the baking dish and bake for at least 15 more minutes.

Allow the cereal to cool then store in an airtight container.

Black bread

We see black bread everywhere in "Clash of Kings" in different meals. We have created a yummier version of that mysterious looking bread. It is a special breakfast treat for the people who are in love with chocolate and GOT.

Serving size: 12

Cooking time: 3 hours 10 minutes

Ingredients:

- Rye flour 1 cup
- Whole wheat flour 1 cup
- Salt 1 ½ teaspoons
- Vegetable oil ¼ cup
- Bread flour 2 cups
- Brown sugar 2 tablespoons
- Dark molasses ¼ cup
- Strong brewed coffee 1 ⅓ cups (room temperature)
- Active dry yeast 2 ½ teaspoons
- Unsweetened cocoa powder 2 tablespoons

Instructions:

Put all the ingredients in the pan of bread machine in the order as suggested by the manufacturer.

Select the cycle of the dough. When the final rise is indicated by the machine, remove dough from it.

Preheat the oven to about 375 F.

Make around 12 dinner rolls from the dough or a single loaf of 9x5 inches.

Let the loaf rise until it doubles in size.

Bake for around 20 minutes in the oven (in case of rolls) and 35 minutes (in case of the loaf).

Cheesy bacon and egg hash

With too much happening every time, we are sure that all the characters in Game of Thrones must need a seriously heavy dose of energy. Here is a breakfast recipe which we think would be perfect for our protagonists. Full of protein and other rich nutrients and the best choice to make a special weekend breakfast.

Serving size: 4

Cooking time: 35 minutes

Ingredients:

- Peeled and cubed potatoes 4 (medium size)
- Diced bacon without fat ½ lb.
- Large eggs 4
- Trimmed and sliced spring onions/shallots 2
- Shredded mozzarella cheese ¼ cup
- Olive oil 2 tablespoons
- Pepper to season

Instructions:

Preheat the oven to about 400 F.

Put potatoes in the skillet, making the single layer.

Spray the cooking spray lightly and then bake for about half an hour while mixing after 15 minutes until it becomes golden and crisp.

Remove it from the oven and add bacon to it. Put back in the oven for 10 minutes and until it becomes crispy.

Make 4-5 wells in hash and put the egg in every well.

Arrange mozzarella around the eggs.

Put the skillet back in the oven until egg whites become set. Serve instantly.

Breakfast strata

Inspired by the dragon eggs from Game of Thrones, this recipe is a perfect egg breakfast for all the fans out there. Make this super cheesy recipe to have a special breakfast with your loved ones on weekends or special occasions. We are sure your taste buds will love this dish.

Serving size: 8

Cooking time: 13 hours 10 minutes

Ingredients:

- Chopped green bell pepper ½ cup
- Shredded cheddar cheese 1 lb.
- Diced fresh mushrooms ½ cup
- Cubed cooked ham 2 cups
- Bread slices sliced into bite-size pieces 9
- Chopped onion ½ cup
- Eggs 8
- Milk 2 cups

Instructions:

Grease a baking dish of about 9x13 inches.

Layer half bread in the dish bottom. Sprinkle the bell pepper and mushrooms on the layer of bread.

Sprinkle only half of the cheddar cheese on it. Then top with the rest of the bread pieces, onions, and ham.

Sprinkle the rest of the cheese.

Whisk the milk and eggs together. Pour it over the whole pan.

Cover it with aluminum foil. Refrigerate for 12 hours.

Preheat oven to about 350 F.

Bake it covered for about 35 minutes. Remove the foil and bake for 15 more minutes and until its top becomes evenly brown.

Egg and cottage cheese breakfast bowl

We see that people of medieval ages eat lots of cheese in different forms and it shows in Game of Thrones also since the story has the same setting. Here is a perfect breakfast recipe for all the GOT fans out there. A combination of eggs and cheese, this breakfast bowl will give you a brilliant start to the day.

Serving size: 1

Cooking time: 10 minutes

Ingredients:

- Cottage cheese ½ cup
- Hard or soft boiled egg 1
- Sliced mini radishes 2
- Green onion and finely chopped chives 1 tablespoon each
- Pepper and salt 1 pinch each
- Sliced cucumber ½ cup
- Sliced avocado half-ripe 1

Instructions:

Place the cottage cheese in a bowl.

Place the cucumber, radish, avocado, and egg on the top.

Garnish it with pepper, salt, and herbs.

Main course

Meat pie

The most popular food all the royal families eat through the series is pies. From pigeon to meat and fish pies, there is an extensive range of pies we see in the GOT. The most classic of all those pies was this meat pie. Try this mouthwatering recipe for a blast of taste and texture.

Serving size: 4

Cooking time: 45 minutes

Ingredients:

- Chopped onion ½ cup
- Garlic powder ½ teaspoon
- Chopped carrot 1
- Cubed cooked or leftover beef 2 cups
- Black pepper ¼ teaspoon
- Margarine 3 tablespoons
- Dried oregano ½ teaspoon
- Single crust pie recipe pastry 1
- Beef broth 1 ¼ cups
- All-purpose flour ⅓ cup
- Frozen green peas 1 cup
- Diced potato 1

Instructions:

Preheat oven to about 425 F.

Roll the recipe pastry and make a circle of 12 inches. Set it aside.

Melt the margarine on medium heat in a saucepan.

Add the onion and potato to it and cook it until the onion becomes soft.

Sprinkle flour into the mixture. Stir for blending.

Season the mixture with garlic powder, black pepper, and oregano.

Pour this mixture into the broth. Add beef, carrot, and peas to it. Bring it to boiling.

Transfer this mixture into a casserole dish. Put the pastry on top.

Cut the slits for the steam. Flute its edges.

Put on the baking sheet. Bake for about half an hour and until the crust becomes golden.

Let it stand for 10 minutes for thickening.

Tourtiere

Do you remember lamprey pies from the Game of Thrones? They were indeed one of the delicious foods ever. We have used our culinary skills and experience to develop a recipe which has similarity with lamprey pie but tastes better than that. This pie recipe tastes divine and we are sure that it will change the impression of lamprey pie for you and everyone.

Serving size: 8

Cooking time: 1 hour 20 minutes

Ingredients:

- Baking potato 1
- Ground black pepper ½ teaspoon
- Ground pork 1 ½ lb.
- Ground allspice 1 tablespoon
- Ground cinnamon ½ teaspoon
- Ground cloves ¼ teaspoon
- Salt ½ teaspoon
- Recipe pastry 1
- Egg 1
- Minced large onion 1
- Paprika ¼ teaspoon
- Water ½ cup

Instructions:

Bake a potato for 30 to 40 minutes and until done in a preheated oven at 400 F. Peel and then mash the potato.

Put the spices, water, onion, ground pork, and potato in a frying pan. Simmer it until thick for an hour.

Meanwhile, prepare the pastry.

Line a plate for pie with the pastry.

Spoon the filling in it and spread evenly. Then cover with the top crust.

Brush the pie with the beaten egg. Sprinkle with the paprika if you like. Cut a steam vent.

Bake at 350 F for 50 minutes and until brown. Serve warm.

Lamb stew

The rancid meat stew in Castle Black was the inspiration behind this flavorful delicacy. Tender lamb meat and just a perfect blend of seasoning make this dish a memorable gourmet experience. Prepare it for a special gathering and let the guests drool over it!

Serving size: 10

Cooking time: 1 hour 30 minutes

Ingredients:

- Olive oil 3 tablespoons
- White sugar a pinch
- Chopped celery stalk 1
- Lamb shoulder (sliced in 2-inch pieces) 3 lb.
- Chopped fresh parsley 1 tablespoon
- Large chopped onion 1
- Dried dill weed ½ teaspoon
- Tomato sauce 1 can
- Hot water 3 cups
- Dried mint ½ teaspoon
- Ground cinnamon a pinch
- Trimmed green beans 2 lb.
- Pepper to taste
- Salt to taste

Instructions:

On medium heat, heat the oil in a big pot.

Sauté celery and onion until golden.

Stir in the lamb. Cook until it is evenly brown.

Add water and tomato sauce, and stir.

Reduce the heat and let it simmer for an hour.

Add the green beans. Then, add dill weed, mint, parsley, pepper, salt, sugar, and cinnamon. Keep cooking until beans become tender.

Serve hot.

Arya Stark's Crab and Lobsters with Mushrooms

Once again, Arya Stark's seafood selling part triggered our imagination and we ended up making this yummy recipe. This recipe is a rich, tasty, and mouthwatering combination of seafood, cheese, and mushroom. Make it to savor the elite taste of these superfoods.

Serving size: 10

Cooking time: 20 minutes

Ingredients:

- Crushed seasoned croutons 1 cup
- Melted butter ¾ cup
- Shredded mozzarella cheese 1 cup
- Fresh mushrooms 1 lb.
- Minced garlic 3 tablespoons
- Drained crabmeat 1 can
- Chopped lobster tail 1 lb.
- Shredded mozzarella cheese ¼ cup

Instructions:

Preheat oven to about 375 F. Use melted butter to brush a big baking sheet.

Put the mushroom caps to make a single layer on the baking sheet.

Take a bowl and then mix garlic, lobster, crabmeat, cheese, butter, and crushed croutons in it.

Spoon the cap of mushrooms where there were stems before.

Bake for 10 minutes in the oven and until they become light brown in color.

Sprinkle extra cheese if you like. Serve hot.

Fried Crab Claws

Seafood and meat are the basic foods in the North because of the tough weather and terrain. We have created a special main course dish taking inspiration from the North-kingdom in Game of Thrones. Crab claws were a part of the menu at the war feast of Queen Cersei also. The crispy coating makes these crab claws a light, main course dish for everybody to relish on.

Serving size: 3

Cooking time: 20 minutes

Ingredients:

- Crab claws ½ lb.
- Corn flour 1 lb.
- Eggs 3
- Salt 1/8 cup
- Pure lard 3 lb.
- Whole milk 2 cups
- Ground black pepper 1/8 cup

Instructions:

Melt the lard in the pot. Keep heating until it is hot.

Stir the salt, pepper, and cornflour in a bowl together.

Beat the milk and eggs in a small bowl. Keep beating the mixture until smoothly blended.

Add the crab claws into the egg wash. After that, transfer it to the cornflour mixture.

In the lard, quickly add the crab claws.

Stir the claws to keep them separate.

Fry these claws until they become light golden brown in color.

Let them sit for a minute and serve hot.

Creamy fish stew

Theon enjoys a creamy fish stew at his welcome home party in Pyke in A Clash of Kings. This soup sounds very edible as compared to the other cringy foods. Our version of creamy fish stew is super delicious and you will love it.

Serving size: 4

Cooking time: 20 minutes

Ingredients:

- Chopped onion 2 cups
- Celery ¼ inch thick slices 1 cup
- Minced garlic cloves 3
- Carrot slices ¼ inch thick 1 cup
- Sliced jalapeño pepper 1
- Dry white wine 1 cup
- Olive oil 1 tablespoon
- Undrained crushed tomatoes 1 can
- Lime wedges
- Cubed and peeled red potato or Yukon gold 2 cups
- Chopped fresh cilantro ½ cup
- Halibut (bite-size pieces) 1 lb.
- Peeled and deveined large shrimp ½ lb.
- Chicken broth 4 cups
- Cilantro sprigs (optional)

Instructions:

Heat the oil in a Dutch oven on medium heat.

Add jalapeño, garlic, celery, carrot, and onion in a pan. Sauté for 5 minutes and until tender.

Stir in the tomatoes, cilantro, wine, potato, and broth. Bring them to boiling.

Reduce heat. Simmer for about 15 minutes and until the potato becomes tender.

Add shrimp and fish and cook for 5 more minutes and until they are done.

Ladle stew into 4 bowls and serve it with the lime wedges.

Garnish the stew with cilantro if desired.

Fish pie

The Stark family rules over the North Kingdom in Games of Thrones and they usually eat seafood. Fish is the most popular seafood and we have made it into this crispy, savory meal. Make it to give a special twist to your pie menu.

Serving size: 4

Cooking time: 55 minutes

Ingredients:

- Chopped garlic cloves 2
- Chopped celery 2 stalks
- Olive oil 3 tablespoons
- Grated Parmesan ½ cup
- Eggs 3
- Peas ½ cup
- Dijon mustard 2 tablespoons
- Packaged and refrigerated mashed potatoes 2 lb.
- Chopped parsley ½ cup
- Milk 1 cup
- Steamed Halibut with Walnuts and Kale
- Sliced scallions 2
- Salt 1 teaspoon
- Chopped carrots 2
- Cooked or raw halibut fillets 2 (0.4 lb.)
- Frozen chopped spinach 1 box

Instructions:

Take a pan and sauté the garlic, carrots, and celery in 3 tbsp oil for about 5 minutes. Then remove it from heat.

Stir in the flaked halibut, salt, Dijon mustard, parsley, Parmesan eggs, peas, spinach, and milk. Pour it into a baking dish.

Mix the mashed potatoes in the scallions.

Spread the mixture on the pie top.

Bake at 400 F for about 40 minutes.

Turnip Greens Stew

Turnips are served with butter in the feast menu in Winterfell. We have elevated the use of turnips in this super-tasty recipe. The ingredients of this dish are different from those of your regular stew which give this a heavenly delicious taste.

Serving size: 10

Cooking time: 40 minutes

Ingredients:

- Chicken broth 3 cups
- Vegetable oil 1 tablespoon
- Drained and rinsed cannellini beans 2 cans
- Frozen chopped turnip greens 2 packages
- Seasoned pepper 1 teaspoon
- Chopped cooked ham 2 cups
- Frozen diced onion 4 cups
- Celery 1 cup
- Green and red bell peppers 4 cups
- Sugar 1 teaspoon

Instructions:

Sauté the ham in a Dutch oven in hot oil on medium heat for about 5 minutes and until light brown in color.

Add the broth and the rest of the ingredients and bring to boiling.

Reduce the heat to a minimum. Simmer for 25 minutes while stirring occasionally in between.

Cersei's Creamy Chestnut soup

In part two of this mind-blowing series, we see Cersei putting a creamy chestnut soup on the table. This soup falls in the main course because of its elite ingredients and exclusive recipe. Try this innovative recipe to see how the royal cuisine of Lannister of Casterly tastes.

Serving size: 6

Cooking time: 20 minutes

Ingredients:

- Chopped onion 1 cup
- Chopped fresh thyme 2 teaspoons
- Ground allspice ¼ teaspoon
- Unsalted chicken stock 3 cups
- Ground ginger ¼ teaspoon
- Cider vinegar 1 tablespoon
- Chopped carrot ½ cup
- All-purpose flour 2 ½ tablespoons
- Apple brandy ¼ cup
- Kosher salt .38 teaspoon
- Unsalted butter 1 tablespoon
- Steamed and peeled chestnuts 1 ½ cups
- Water 1 cup
- Black pepper .38 teaspoon

Instructions:

In the saucepan, heat the butter on medium heat.

Add the carrot and onion in butter and cook for about 10 minutes.

Stir in the allspice, ginger, thyme, and chestnuts and cook for a minute.

Add the apple brandy and cook it until it is reduced to half.

Combine the flour and chicken stock. Stir it using a whisk.

Add the stock mixture, then a cup of water into the pan.

Bring it to boiling, then reduce the heat. Cover it and simmer for about 12 minutes.

Place the mixture into the blender. Blend it until smooth.

Return the blended mixture to the pan and cook for 3 minutes on low heat.

Stir in the pepper, vinegar, and salt. Serve hot.

White beans and bacon

This recipe is extremely special for the GOT fans because it comes from the special cuisine of Westeros. The original recipe had butter but we have made this version almost fat-free. Try this healthy, yummy, and royal recipe from your favorite series to build your bond stronger.

Serving size: 4

Cooking time: 40 minutes

Ingredients:

- Chopped onion 1 cup
- Chopped escarole 6 cups
- Freshly ground black pepper ¼ teaspoon
- Sugar 1 teaspoon
- Chopped bacon slices 2
- Thinly sliced garlic clove 1
- Chicken broth (fat-free) 1 can
- Salt ¼ teaspoon
- Rinsed and drained cannellini beans 1 can

Instructions:

In a saucepan, cook the bacon until crisp on medium heat.

Use a slotted spoon to remove the bacon from the pan. Reserve about 2 tsp drippings in the pan. And then set the bacon aside.

Add the onion to the pan. Cook for 12 minutes and until golden brown in color while stirring occasionally.

Add the garlic then cook for about 2 minutes while stirring.

Add the escarole, then cook it for about 2 minutes and until the escarole wilts while stirring constantly.

Add chicken broth, pepper, salt, and sugar and cook for 15 minutes and until escarole becomes tender.

Add the beans and cook for two minutes and until heated thoroughly. Sprinkle it with the bacon.

Mushroom Pie

Did you notice that in Game of Thrones, pigeon pie was a special feast recipe for the royals? This recipe consists of simple ingredients but the cooking method gives you a blast of taste.

Serving size: 12

Cooking time: 1 hour

Ingredients:

- Olive oil 1 tablespoon
- Chopped bacon slices 4
- Shredded Swiss cheese 1 cup
- Chopped fresh dill 1 teaspoon
- Sliced fresh mushrooms 1 package
- Pepper and salt to taste
- Chopped large onion 1
- Thawed frozen puff pastry 1 package
- Heavy cream ¾ cup
- Beaten egg 1

Instructions:

First, preheat oven to about 350 F.

In a skillet, heat the olive oil on medium heat.

Add the bacon, onion, and mushrooms to the saucepan. Cook them and stir for 5 minutes and until the vegetables become tender.

Reduce heat to the medium flame. Add the dill and cheese. Then keep cooking for 10 minutes.

Remove from heat. Stir the Swiss cheese into it.

On an oiled baking sheet, put a puff pastry sheet. Pour the filling of mushroom on its top. Then cover it with another sheet. Press the edges together for sealing well. Make a few holes on top using a fork.

Brush the top with the beaten egg.

Bake for 40 minutes in the oven and until golden brown in color. Cool and cut into small squares for serving.

Desserts

Lemon cake

King Joffrey and other monarchs used to eat lemon cakes in Game of Thrones. We wanted the GOT fans to savor this mouthwatering dessert in the best possible version. The perfect balance of sweet taste with a tangy lemon flavour makes it an irresistible food.

Serving size: 10

Cooking time: 45 minutes

Ingredients:

- Butter ½ cup
- All-purpose flour 1 ½ cups
- Lemon zest 1 tablespoon
- Baking powder 1 ¾ teaspoons
- Vanilla extract 2 teaspoons
- White sugar 1 cup
- Lemon juice 1 tablespoon
- Milk ¾ cup
- Eggs 2

Instructions:

Preheat oven to about 350 F.

Grease a baking pan of 9 inches.

Beat the butter and sugar in a bowl with the electric mixer. Beat until the mixture gets fluffy and light.

Beat the eggs and vanilla extract in it.

Stir in the baking powder and flour together in a different bowl. Add it to the creamed mixture.

Pour in the lemon juice, lemon zest, and milk. Mix it until you get a really smooth batter.

Spoon the batter in the greased pan.

Bake the batter in the oven for 35 minutes.

Cersei's War Feast Cheesecake

Queen Cersei served the soldiers with goat cheese along with many other foods at the war feast. Sweet dishes and celebrations have a very strong connection. This delicious recipe combines the celebration from GOT and the sweetness of cheesecake together.

Serving size: 16

Cooking time: 4 hours 15 minutes

Ingredients:

- Heavy cream 2 cups
- White sugar 1 cup
- Cream cheese ½ lb.
- Oval butter sandwich cookies with the chocolate filling 4 packages
- Raspberry pie filling 1 can

Instructions:

Put the sugar and cream cheese together in a bowl and set it aside.

In a different bowl, whip the cream until some stiff peaks are formed.

Fold in the whipped cream in the mixture of cream cheese.

Take a springform pan of 9 inches and line its sides and bottom with the cookies.

Pour the mixture of cheesecake (only half) on the cookies.

Top it with half of the raspberry filling. Spread it evenly.

Make another cookie layer over the raspberry layer and repeat the same with raspberry and cheese layers.

Chill the cake in the refrigerator for about 4 hours before serving.

Apple pie

Baked apples were part of the war feast menu of the Lannister Dynasty. This apple pie is the refined version of baked apples from Game of Thrones. Our version is the most delicious apple pie recipe you would ever taste.

Serving size: 8

Cooking time: 40 minutes

Ingredients:

- Butter 1 tablespoon
- Milk 4 tablespoons
- Lemon zest ½ teaspoon
- Ground nutmeg ¼ teaspoon
- All-purpose flour 2 tablespoon
- Ground cinnamon ½ teaspoon
- Thinly sliced apples 7 cups
- Lemon juice 2 teaspoons
- Recipe pastry 1
- White sugar ¾ cup

Instructions:

Preheat the oven to about 425 F.

Mix the flour, lemon peel, nutmeg, cinnamon, and sugar in a bowl together.

In a 9-inch deep pie pan, line a crust. Put 1/3 apples in the crust of the pie. Sprinkle the mixture of sugar and keep doing the same until it is done. Sprinkle two teaspoons of lemon juice. Dot it with butter.

Place the second crust on the filling and then smooth the edges. Make vents in the upper crust, and to give it a glazed look by brushing it with milk.

Bake it for 40 minutes at 425 F.

Mini marzipan cakes

A massive range of cakes was part of the elite's menu in Game of Thrones. Instead of regular cream or chocolate cakes, this recipe presents you with the most flavorful mini treats. You can try them for your special and most formal events to make them memorable.

Serving size: 6

Cooking time: 1 hour

Ingredients:

- Marzipan 0.22 lb.
- Eggs 4
- Sugar 0.22 lb.
- Vanilla sugar 1 packet
- Pastry flour 0.22 lb.
- Baking powder 2 teaspoons
- Ground almonds 0.22 lb.

For filling

- Mixed fruit jam 0.28 lb.
- Whipping cream 0.88 lb.
- Sugar 0.11 lb.
- Bourbon vanilla and cream stabilizer each packet

For garnish

- Marzipan 0.22 lb.
- Sifted powdered sugar 0.11 lb.
- Different food coloring
- Toasted chopped almonds 0.11 lb.

Instructions:

Beat an egg and marzipan until smooth.

Add and mix the rest of the ingredients for the cake until combined.

Line the baking sheet using parchment paper and fill it with batter.

Smooth the batter surface. Bake it in the oven for about 20 minutes at 350 F.

Invert sponge cake on the wire rack. Cut it into 6 circles. Cut every circle to make three horizontal layers.

To make the filling, take the jam and spread it over the middle and bottom of the cake layers. Then stack these cakes together.

Whip the heavy cream. Then add vanilla to it and beat until stiff. Spread the cream on the cakes and chill.

To garnish, knead powdered sugar and marzipan. Tint the mixture with the food coloring.

Roll it out thinly. Decorate the cake with it. Sprinkle with the toasted almonds for serving.

Cherry tarts

We have picked this unique recipe that melts in your mouth and makes a perfect dessert for all the sweet tooth out there. Let's try it today!

Serving size: 12

Cooking time: 30 minutes

Ingredients:

- Pitted fresh cherries 4 cups
- Cornstarch ¼ cup
- Softened margarine or butter ¼ cup
- Water 1 tablespoon
- Almond extract 1 teaspoon
- Sugar 1 ½ cups
- Baked tart shells (1 3/4-inch) 48

Instructions:

Combine the sugar and cherries in a saucepan.

Cook it on medium heat while stirring continuously for 15 minutes and until cherries become soft.

Dissolve the cornstarch into water. Blend it well.

Add cornstarch water into the mixture of cherry and bring it to boiling.

Reduce the heat and cook while constantly stirring and until the mixture becomes bubbly and thickened.

Remove it from heat. Stir in the almond extract and butter and cool.

Spoon about 2 teaspoons of the cherry filling in every tart shell.

Transfer to the serving platter. Enjoy.

Cream Snow Cupcakes

Snow has yummy, and cream adds a rich taste and texture to every recipe. This recipe takes your dessert game up to the next level. Give your taste buds a yummy treat with this mouthwatering recipe inspired by the snow from GOT.

Serving size: 24

Cooking time: 1 hour 39 minutes

Ingredients:

- Egg whites 4
- Jell-O Lemon Instant Pudding 1 package
- Vegetable oil 2 tablespoons
- Softened butter ¼ cup
- White cake mix 1 package
- Softened Philadelphia Brick Cream Cheese 1 package
- Lemon juice 2 tablespoons
- Icing sugar 3 ¾ cups
- Water 1 cup

Instructions:

Preheat the oven to about 350 F.

Beat the white cake mix, instant pudding, eggs, water, and vegetable oil in a bowl. Mix all the ingredients using the mixer for a minute on low speed until the dry ingredients get moistened.

Then beat the mixture on a medium speed for 2 minutes.

Spoon the natter into 24 muffin cups.

Bake the cupcakes for 25 minutes and until well baked.

Cool the cupcakes in their pans for about 10 minutes. Remove the cakes on wire racks. Then cool down completely.

Beat the lemon juice, butter, and cheese in a bowl using a mixer until the mixture blends well.

Add the sugar gradually, and beat it well after every addition. Then spread the mixture onto the cupcakes and enjoy.

Conclusion

The craze of Games of Throne has taken the world by storm and fans want it everywhere around them. Our passion for food and Game of Thrones unites and results in this magically impressive cookbook.

The recipes are from all the seven kingdoms and contain exclusive ingredients from Game of Thrones. You can make any of these recipes to make your GOT parties more exclusive. Enjoy!

About the Author

Contemporary Caribbean cuisine had never tasted so good before Rene Reed came into the scene. With about twenty years dedicated to building up a budding culinary career, Rene has worked in various top-end restaurants, hotels, and resorts as the head chef. Her dive into the food industry started in Michigan, where she trained with some of the best chefs on the block. Rene was an accountant at a top firm but didn't feel a sense of accomplishment at the end of the day. Something was missing, and although Rene didn't know it at that time, the answer was right under her nose.

She discovered how relaxed and happy she felt when she was trying to whip up something in the kitchen for her family. To her, cooking was equivalent to vacation time, where she could do whatever she wanted. Encouraged by her family and loved ones, Rene quit her job and started her culinary training in earnest. Her efforts yielded so much success as she built up a network that propelled her to key positions all around the industry.

She specializes in exceptional Caribbean cuisine while also adding that unique Rene touch to every menu as much as she can.

Author's Afterthoughts

Thank you for taking out time to read my work. I put in all those hours, and I'm super glad that you found it worthy enough to download. I would love to ask for one more thing, and that is your feedback. It will be lovely to know your thoughts on the contents of the book. Was it worth your time? Would you like me to change anything for my subsequent books? I'll love to hear them all.

Thanks!

Rene Reed